THE ART OF THE
UNIGNORABLE EMAIL

THE ART OF THE
UNIGNORABLE EMAIL

How to combine AI and EQ to win
the battle of the inbox

David Pullan & Sarah Jane McKechnie

Book Interior and E-book Design by Amit Dey (amitdey2528@gmail.com)

To find out more about our authors and books visit:

www.intellectualperspective.com

TABLE OF CONTENTS

PRAISE FOR THE ART OF THE UNIGNORABLE EMAIL

A must-read for anyone who's ever typed 'just touching base' and immediately regretted it. It is practical, punchy, smart, structured and mercifully free of corporate nonsense. This isn't just a book about email, it's a masterclass in influence. If you lead people, manage stakeholders, or just want your messages to land, read this. Then make your team read it too.

Flora Spink - Group Head of Culture and Engagement - Aviva

This is a genius handbook that will change your reputation at work. David Pullan and Sarah Jane McKechnie show you not only how to craft emails that land and get the responses you need, but also what type of email to write when. Packed with brilliant, actionable guidance and smart shortcuts, this slender but incredibly wise book takes you from email hell to nirvana. If you want to be known as the person who gets stuff done and cement your reputation as someone who is smart and on top of things, look no further.

Charlotte Otter – author of Amazon Bestseller We Need New Leaders and podcast host of Speech Bubbles

The pandemic of endless communication that just doesn't cut through is over. This brilliant book is the first step to ensure you never send something purposeless again. Consider yourself fully vaccinated against emails that are too long and too complex.

Susie Ashfield - Speech and presentation coach and
bestselling author of *Just F**king Say It*

We all hope people read our emails. Most don't. This book shows you why - and what to do about it. With clarity, humour and practical tips, David and Sarah Jane turn email into real communication - not just inbox noise. Their DNA framework is sharp, simple and endlessly usable. If you write emails (i.e. if you breathe), read this. Then notice how many people actually reply.

Goran Serdarevic
- Director at Frontier Economics

I can never fail to be impressed by the energy, wisdom and fun that David and Sarah Jane put into everything they do. They have done it once again!

Lee Anderson
- Co-Founder Specialist Risk Group

Brimming with tips, easy-to-use structures and great examples. Especially valuable is the guidance on adapting for different audiences - a skill most email writers never truly master.

Chris Fenning
- Communication skills author and instructor

This book will not only increase your response rate but position you as a proactive and solution-driven professional. It should be part of the toolbox of any seasoned manager.

Simon Pannatier
- Project Manager and Consultant - a-connect

WHO THIS BOOK IS FOR

This book is for anyone caught in the middle.

You might be a manager caught in the "sandwich generation" of corporate life where you have to influence up to senior leadership and coordinate down to your team, sometimes without any formal authority in either direction.

You might be a project leader who is constantly bringing different departments, personalities and priorities together to deliver results that matter.

You might be a cross-functional coordinator who has to get marketing, sales, IT, finance and HR to care as much about a project as you do.

You might be a Chief of Staff or Executive Assistant who has to craft communications for your boss knowing that the tone and structure need to be exactly right because the stakes are high and everyone's watching.

If you are someone who recognises that internal emails operate in an arena worthy of Gladiator II and one false slip could make or break a project, relationship or career opportunity - then this book is for you.

And never forget that the first blow your message will receive will come from the Sword of Ignorability.

The harsh reality of all communication in our increasingly busy world is that everyone is looking for an excuse to say, "This doesn't affect me. I'll focus on something more relevant or urgent."

Which means your email is in a battle for that scarcest of commodities - attention.

Miss the mark and you might not get another chance to influence that critical stakeholder.

Hit the mark and you will guarantee engagement as you set the narrative tone for any subsequent conversation.[1]

All of which will shape your reputation as a leader, collaborator and problem-solver.

If you've ever stared at a blank screen knowing that your next move could spell the difference between project success and career stagnation you're in the right place.

You've suffered the pain. Now master the gain.

Welcome to the future of your sent box.

ENDNOTES

1. If you'd like to know more about this you should take a look at "High Output Management" by Andrew S. Grove and our original book "The DNA of Engagement® - a story based approach to building trust and influencing change".

WHY MOST EMAILS FAIL AND WHAT TO DO ABOUT IT

It's hell out there

It's Monday morning and your first day back from holiday.

The sound of cicadas is still ringing in your ears as you turn on the coffee and open your inbox.

Dear God! 987 digital diatribes and ALL of them marked urgent.

You scan the sender list and subject line to see which ones you can ignore or deflect and which ones need immediate attention.

There's one from your boss. **"Morrison deadline moved - emergency meeting 9am Monday"**. That needs a reply before the Nespresso machine is even lukewarm.

There are a dozen from the client with variations of **"Touching base on what we discussed last week when you get a minute"**. Could be important but you can triage those after the second flat white.

And then there's a long list of updates, notifications and vague requests where everyone is CC'd and you can feel your brain glucose draining away at the thought of the time it will take to clear the backlog.

Sound familiar?

Well here's the thing - email hell is an equal opportunities pain point.

You are subjected to it. And your emails get caught in it.

One in four people say they suffer from miscommunication several times a day which leads to increased stress and decreased productivity.[1] And business professionals like you report that they waste approximately 28% of their working week reading, organising and responding to the mess of their inbox.[2]

Is it any wonder that many business emails fail to land effectively?

The added challenge of the AI inbox guardians

In an attempt to counteract this overwhelm we now have AI tools which promise to "help us" claw back some precious time.

These housekeeping bots stand guard over the inbox, intercepting messages to filter, prioritise and auto-reply before emails ever reach the intended human recipient.

The result? Your carefully crafted messages must now run the double gauntlet of an AI gatekeeper and the fleeting attention span of whoever's left on the other side.

Send anything that smacks of the generic or template and an AI guardian will judge your email to be ignorable and whisk it away faster than a beefburger at a vegan barbecue.

The bar has been raised and if you want your message to stand out there are some simple mistakes you need to watch out for.

The hills on which business emails die

Business emails fail for five fundamental reasons.

1. They're Structured Backwards

   Too many emails begin with background informa-tion, context and details and bury the main point somewhere in the middle or at the end. By the time your reader gets to what matters, they've already pressed delete or moved on.

2. They Don't Have a "Why"

   The first question your reader asks when they see your email pop up is, "Why should I care about this?" Unfortunately most emails focus on what the sender cares about without addressing what matters to the recipient. If you don't close the reader/care loop you're in danger of being sent to the bin.

3. Too Long; Did Not Read[3]

   There have been studies that show the sweet spot for business email length is between 50-125 words. These are the ones that get a response. But the average business email is over 250 words.[4]

4. They Lack Personalisation

   If your email is about a current or future relationship then make it personal. The test to give yourself is "Would my reader notice if their name or circumstances were replaced with someone else's?"

5. They Don't Lead to Action

   If your recipient doesn't know what they're meant to do with the information in your email you run the risk you won't get a reply. A clear request will lead to tangible action.

And as AI tools get better and better at judging which messages should take top priority, these five points will only become steeper paths on the hill that you climb.

The DNA approach to becoming unignorable

So, now we come to it: the reason you've spent your hard earned money on this book.

What you are about to read is a simple, repeatable structure augmented by the "heavy lifting muscle" of AI that will dramatically increase your engagement scores for every email you send.

We'll get to the muscle in good time.

But let's start with that structure, The DNA of Engagement®.

The DNA is a proven communication approach based on how humans process information and make decisions.

At its core, it consists of three key elements:

1. **Dream** - We identify what we want
2. **Nightmare** - We establish what's getting in the way
3. **Action** - We decide what to do about it

It could be as simple as making the decision to cook an omelette for breakfast. But then discovering that you don't have any eggs. So, you knock on your neighbour's door and ask to borrow two that you will replace that evening.

Or as complex as wanting to get various countries to agree on climate change policies. But then realising that burden-share, transition costs and economic dependencies are a major hurdle. So, you arrange a global conference to negotiate the way forward.

From the micro to the macro we humans are driven by our DNA. You can think of it as the human story world.

This story world is a never ending narrative where we all interpret our existence from our own perspective and place ourselves as the main player.

When you realise this you will unlock a secret that you can apply to your emails, or indeed any communication channel.

You will be on the verge of creating a powerful structure that pulls your reader into your way of thinking rather than pushing information onto them. And as we said in our original book, if you try and push something onto someone you run the risk that they will push back.[5]

This is what DNA communication looks like in a nutshell.

1. You start by connecting to what matters to your reader through specific, personalised understanding of their story world. Their **DREAM**

2. This creates immediate engagement and earns you the permission to bring up the relevant challenges that threaten their dream. The **NIGHTMARE**

3. Which will lead to you suggesting collaborative solutions and making specific requests that will overcome the nightmare and achieve their dream. The **ACTION**

Simple as that.

But the real beauty of the DNA framework lies in the fact that it can be inverted to create different effects according to the context and needs of the recipient.

Here are the inversions we'll be looking at.

- **DNA (Dream, Nightmare, Action)** - For building rapport and trust

- **NAD (Nightmare, Action, Dream)** - For addressing urgent issues
- **AND (Action, Nightmare, Dream)** - For creating collaboration
- **NDA (Nightmare, Dream, Action)** - For making the case for change

We'll also throw in a bonus emergency structure called **ROAD** but we won't spoil the surprise of that one.

All of these inversions have an emotional strength and depth that will conquer AI and engage humans whether you are communicating up, down or across . We'll be exploring all of them in depth.

Which begs the question, "How should I use this book?"

How to use this book

In the following chapters you're going to learn exactly how to use each DNA inversion to transform your email communication.

Each chapter will give you:

- Step-by-step guidance on when and how to use each inversion
- Before-and-after examples that show the inversions in action
- Templates to make the inversions quick and easy[6]
- Pro tips for taking the inversions to the next level

- Crucial stumbling blocks to avoid if you want to become unignorable

And at the end of the book we are going to give you three free bonuses.

1. A full list of all the templates
2. AI prompts for all of the inversions
3. An app to help you choose which inversion will suit which occasion

Phew! We're packing a lot into these pages.

Of course, we hope you read the whole book from cover to cover to get a full picture of what is possible.

But if you want to jump directly to the section that addresses your most pressing email challenge then don't let us stop you.

In fact, here's a quick diagnostic flow chart to make that jumping even easier.

What's the PRIMARY purpose of this email?

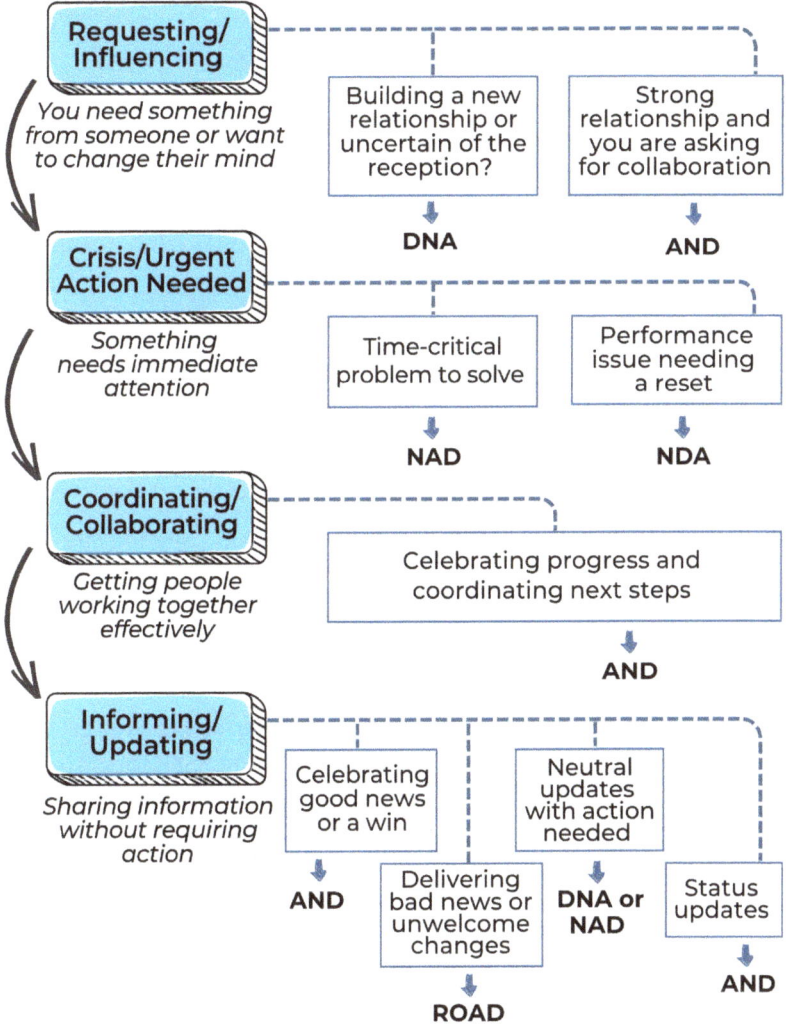

Requesting/ Influencing

You need something from someone or want to change their mind

Building a new relationship or uncertain of the reception?	Strong relationship and you are asking for collaboration
DNA	**AND**

Crisis/Urgent Action Needed

Something needs immediate attention

Time-critical problem to solve	Performance issue needing a reset
NAD	**NDA**

Coordinating/ Collaborating

Getting people working together effectively

Celebrating progress and coordinating next steps

AND

Informing/ Updating

Sharing information without requiring action

Celebrating good news or a win		Neutral updates with action needed	
AND	Delivering bad news or unwelcome changes	**DNA or NAD**	Status updates
	ROAD		**AND**

We are sure that this list is neither mutually exclusive nor completely exhaustive but, as you can see, the ways to use the frameworks are many and varied.[7]

And whichever way you choose to use them we make one promise.

With a bit of intentional application you'll master a communication approach that will not only make your emails unignorable but elevate your entire professional reputation.

The only way is up

At four points in the book you are going to come across a box like this.

We have called it "The only way is up" because as a fully paid-up member of the corporate "sandwich generation" there will be times when you have no option but to send an email to someone who sits anywhere from one rung above you, right up to the board.

And those emails will need some special skills to address three big pressures that come into play when someone reaches senior leadership.

1. They have less time than ever before
2. They need to focus on the organisational big picture
3. They are constantly threatened by cognitive overload through the sheer weight of information

This has a direct bearing on their communication preferences.

They generally want:

- Bottom line up front communication (BLUF for you U.S. military fans)
- Clear material that is ready to help them make decisions
- Business impact analysis over lengthy process detail

And they want all of this quickly because … well, time pressures

In all four of these boxes we'll give you an example of each inversion in action and point out the key differences.

You'll find your first one at the end of the following section where we'll look at how to apply the foundational DNA structure to your emails.

A few thoughts on subject lines

Before we dive into the DNA we need to have a quick chat about subject lines.

Assuming that you've bypassed the bot, the subject line is the first thing that the attention poor gatekeeper in your reader's brain will test to see whether your carefully crafted message gets opened or ignored.

So, let's start with a few sobering truths about that gatekeeper.

Recent research suggests that 64% of people check their emails on their mobile devices.[8] And 58% do it first thing in the morning before they've even glanced at social media or the news.[9]

In short, your words are fighting for the gatekeeper's attention when it is pressed for time and wanting to move on. That gatekeeper is ruthless.

To avoid the risk of being ignored you need to start by crafting a subject line that says one thing to the gatekeeper, "You need to open this NOW!"

This will need four key elements.

1. A punchy six to ten words
2. Relevant and valuable personalisation
3. Clear language
4. A three-tier approach

The three-tier approach is about tailoring your subject line to the needs of your recipient and where they sit in relation to you within your organisation.

Heading Up: Focus on strategic impact, results or risks.

Heading Down: Emphasise clarity, action, and support.

Heading Across: Highlight collaboration, shared goals or mutual benefits.

Throughout the book we'll give you examples of these and we'll make sure that your AI prompts help you create unignorable subject lines.

But here's a good analogue technique you can apply at any time. It's called The Monday Morning Test.

Before you press send on any email, put yourself in the shoes of your reader.

Imagine that it is Monday morning and they've been up all night looking after their sick dog.

Read your subject line out loud and ask yourself, "Would I open this one?"

Be brutally honest.

Because it won't matter how many brilliant insights you've had about key challenges and collaborative solutions if the first thing your recipient reads is **"Re: Re: Re: Re: Budget – just touching base on next steps – IMPORTANT FOR EVERYONE!!!"**

Now, let's get on with the DNA.

ENDNOTES

1.   The 2024 State of Business Communication Report (2024) https://www.grammarly.com/business/learn/introducing-2024-state-of-business-communication/ (Accessed July 2025)

2.   Plummer, Matt. (2019) How to Spend Way Less Time on Email Every Day   https://hbr.org/2019/01/how-to-spend-way-less-time-on-email-every-day (Accessed June 2025)

3.   TL;DR as the cool kids say. On this note, a friend of ours was once told by a senior leader that if an email needs scrolling it should have been a meeting.

4.   Hubspot (2025) The Ideal Length of a Sales Email, Based on 40 Million Emails https://blog.hubspot.com/sales/ideal-length-sales-email (Accessed July 2025)

5.   Newton's Third Law applied to emails.

6.   We know. We know. AI hates templates. These are just 'How-to' guides that you should adapt to your voice and context.

7.   Thank you Barbara Minto and Aristotle for the MECE Framework

8.   CloudHQ (2025) Workplace Email Statistics 2025: Usage, Productivity, Trends https://blog.cloudhq.net/workplace-email-statistics/ (Accessed July 2025)

9.   Porsche Group Media (2025) 100 Compelling Email Statistics for 2025 https://porchgroupmedia.com/blog/100-compelling-email-statistics-to-inform-your-strategy-in-2023/ (Accessed July 2025)

THE "DNA" STRUCTURE - YOUR GATEWAY TO RAPPORT AND TRUST

When DNA is your best friend

As President Teddy Roosevelt said, "Nobody cares how much you know until they know how much you care."[1]

This is definitely the case when you are building initial rapport or trying to repair a relationship that has gone wrong.

Your recipient will only care about the problems and solutions you need to bring up if they first know that you have understood where *they* are coming from.

This makes the DNA structure the perfect approach when you need to:

- Build trust with someone new
- Get buy-in from a sceptical stakeholder
- Ask for resources without sounding demanding

The DNA structure works because it follows a pattern of connection, conflict, consequence.

- It connects to the reader's agenda (Dream)
- It flags up the conflict and challenges to their agenda (Nightmare),
- Then proposes solutions as a consequence (Action).

It's like meeting someone at a conference, connecting to what they're interested in, empathising and giving insight into the challenges they might face ... and only then giving them your contact details and suggesting a coffee.

Much more effective than downing your wine, shoving your card in their face and screaming, "LET'S DO BUSINESS."

The anatomy of a DNA email

Let's break down exactly how you can craft an email that builds rapport and gets the results you need

1. DREAM section (25-40 words)

Start by showing that you understand what matters to your reader. This isn't about flattery - it's about genuinely connecting to their priorities and goals.

Your goal: To get them nodding in agreement and thinking, "This person gets it."

Key elements:

- Make sure you reference a specific conversation or priority they've mentioned
- Connect to a business goal they care about
- Use "AND" as the word to link to the positive future benefits they want
- Avoid any corporate waffle - a definite red flag to a bot

2. NIGHTMARE section (15-30 words)

Now you introduce the challenge or obstacle with that three letter Anglo-Saxon dynamo "BUT".

"But" creates productive friction by injecting their brain with a quick shot of cortisol and dopamine that gives your email urgency and makes it worthy of more attention.

Your goal: To create enough concern to make them want to hear your solution but not so much that they call their therapist.

Key elements:

- Use "BUT" to create a surprising and high stakes pivot
- Be specific about an obstacle that will get in the way of their success
- Support this with concrete data[2]
- Keep this section brief and punchy

3. ACTION section (25-40 words)

Now get to your solution with "THEREFORE" or "SO" and map out your suggested approach or request.

Your goal: To give them a clear path forward that feels collaborative rather than demanding.

Key elements:

- Use "THEREFORE" or "SO" to bridge into your solution
- Emphasise a collaborative approach with words like "we" and "together"
- Make the next steps specific and actionable
- End with a clear and simple call to action

DNA in action: before and after

Nothing is going to show you the power of DNA better than a before and after comparison.

Before:

Subject: Quick question I need answering - just touching base when you get a minute!

Hi Marcus,

Hope this finds you well and that everything is going smoothly at your end. I wanted to reach out about something that's been on my mind lately.

I've been thinking about our marketing campaign situation and I have to say it's been quite a journey! As you know, we've been working on various initiatives across multiple departments and there have been some interesting developments that I thought might be worth discussing at some point.

I was wondering if we could potentially schedule a meeting sometime soon? I don't want to add to a packed schedule, but I feel like it might be beneficial to have a conversation about where we're at with the Q3 marketing campaign.

There are some things that have come up that I think we should probably address sooner rather than later, though I don't want to alarm you unnecessarily.

I'm fairly flexible with my schedule, so I can probably accommodate most times. Tuesday and Thursday afternoons are generally good for me if they work for you.

Let me know when you have a moment!

Looking forward to hearing from you.

Best regards and speak soon,
Sarah

After:

Subject: Customer acquisition 27% boost - Tuesday input needed

Hi Marcus,

I need 20 minutes in your calendar next Tuesday or Thursday afternoon for your input re: the Q3 optimisation goals you mentioned in last week's leadership meeting.

You said that increasing customer acquisition is our top priority and that if we hit our targets we'll put the team in a good position at bonus time. I couldn't agree more.

But our current approach to the campaign is tracking 18% below target based on Q2 results. This could put both your acquisition goals and the team's bonus at risk.

So, I'd like to show you three optimisation strategies that I've seen deliver a 27% lift in similar situations.

I'll speak to your PA about the best time for that call.

Best,
Sarah

What changed?

1. The subject line was immediately relevant, specific and value-focused
2. The Dream section connected to Marcus's stated priority
3. The Nightmare section built urgency with specific data
4. The Action section offered concrete value and a clear, easy request
5. The call to action was specific and bookended the whole email
6. The entire message was personalised and focused on Marcus's priorities

How to craft your own DNA emails

Step 1: Research your reader

Before you even lay a finger on the keyboard, think about these things.

- What is your reader's top priority right now?

- What will success mean to them in the future?
- What previous interactions can you reference?

Remember: The best emails aren't cobbled together - they're finely engineered.

Step 2: Connect to their dream

Start with a specific reference to what they care about.

- When we spoke last week you mentioned ...
- I know your team has been focused on ...
- Given your goal of increasing market share this quarter ...

Then use "AND" to link to a specific positive outcome they care about. For example:

- AND achieving this would put us ahead of the competition.
- AND this would significantly improve team morale.
- AND getting this right will be a major PR coup.

Step 3: Introduce the nightmare

Use "BUT" followed by a concise statement of the challenge:

- BUT the current timeline is creating significant risks.
- BUT the recent data shows a concerning trend.
- BUT our competitors are moving quickly in this space.

Support this with specific data if at all possible:

- Conversion rates have dropped by 15%.
- Three key stakeholders have said they are worried.
- At the moment we're 12 days behind schedule.

Step 4: Present your action

Bridge with "THEREFORE" or "SO" to your collaborative solution:

- THEREFORE/SO, I'd like to propose a revised approach.
- THEREFORE/SO, I suggest we consider these three options.
- THEREFORE/SO, I've developed a solution that addresses these concerns.

End with a clear call to action that is easy to respond to.

- What time on Thursday is best for a 15 minute call to talk about this?
- What's the best way to share the full details of the plan for your review?
- I'm free for a call tomorrow after 2pm. When would suit you?

DNA email templates for common scenarios

Remember: you can download all the templates that you see in this book when you sign up for your bonus extras at www.thestoryspotters.com.

Requesting resources

```
Subject: [Their priority]solution ready -[time-
frame] input needed

Hi [Name],

When I saw you [reference a specific meeting/
conversation], you emphasised the importance of
[their priority] and how achieving [specific met-
ric/outcome] would mean [benefit that matters to
them]. I fully agree with this.

But the current [limitation/challenge] is cre-
ating a significant obstacle, with [specific data
point] showing that [impact on their priority].

So, I'd like to suggest that we [name the spe-
cific solution]. This would [bridge back to their
desired future benefit] and only require [reason-
able resource commitment].

When are you free for [specific length of time] on
[days] to look at the details?

Best,
[Your name]
```

Proposing a new idea

Subject: [their goal]acceleration plan - 15 minute overview ready

Hi [Name],

I know you and your team are focused on [their priority] and that successfully [achieving their goal] would mean [specific positive outcome they care about].

But I'm concerned that the [current approach/situation] is causing [specific challenge] based on [data/observation]. This could limit our ability to [achieve their priority].

So, I've developed [solution] that could [specific benefit aligned with their goals]. What's the best way to share a brief overview?

I could send a one-page summary or discuss for 15 minutes on [name the days].

Best,
[Your name]

Building a new relationship

Subject: [event]follow up - [missed opportunity topic] discussion

Hi [Name],

It was great [meeting you/speaking with you] at [specific event]. I found what you said about [the topic they discussed] particularly valuable. And your approach to [something they care about] aligns with everything I've been thinking about [relevant area].

But I realise I didn't get a chance to talk to you about [missed opportunity] which feels increasingly important given [industry trend/challenge].

So, I wondered if we could find 20-minutes for a call to pick this up.

When would suit you over the next couple of weeks?

Best,
[Your name]

Pro tips for next-level DNA emails

Personalise to beat the AI

The AI inbox "bouncers" are throwing out generic mes-sages like they're a drunk at a disco stinking of Sauvage.[3] To stop this try these things:

- Reference specific meetings, dates or conversations
- Mention details that only you would know
- Avoid clichéd phrases and template language[4]

Keep it scannable and mobile friendly

Most people skim emails on the move before they decide whether to read them properly.

- Use short paragraphs (2-3 sentences maximum)
- Put key information in bold ... but sparingly
- Break multiple items into bullet points
- Make sure your call to action stands alone

Remember this: These tips will help you in all the inversions of the DNA. And you should keep them in mind when it comes to adding your human heart to the AI muscle that we'll look at later.

When DNA goes wrong

The DNA is a great structure. But even the greatest structures can fail if you overlook the details.

Don't make these common mistakes.

Fake understanding

Pretending to understand someone's priorities when you don't is worse than not trying. If you're not sure what matters to them, do your homework.

The too hot/too cold nightmare

Like Goldilocks you need to get your nightmare section just right. It needs to have enough tension that it creates interest and a drive to action. But not so much that it puts the reader into paralysis or anger.

Vague actions

"Let's meet to discuss" without context or specifics is a waste of everyone's time.

What exactly do you want to discuss? When do you want to discuss it? What decisions need to be made? Be specific.

And remember that "Are you free?" risks a yes or no answer.

"I've spoken to your EA and put a call in for 20 minutes on Wednesday. Let me know if that becomes a problem?" takes the burden off them to find a time and gives them leeway to make the final decision.

Making it about you

The moment your Dream section focuses on your needs rather than theirs you've lost the DNA advantage. Always keep their priorities central.

The only way is up

Managing up with DNA: Getting senior leadership buy-in

As we said earlier, when you communicate upward, senior leaders need to know that you understand the bigger picture.

The key to a successful **DNA** upward email, particularly if you are in the early stages of building the relationship, is to make sure that you connect your request to any strategic priorities.

Connection before correction is the phrase we use.

The main things you need to do with a **DNA** upward email are:

- Lead with business impact, not process details
- Refer to market pressures or competitive threats
- Make the ROI clear and quantifiable

Here is an example **DNA** template asking for more budget from a senior leader.

Subject: [Strategic goal] budget request - [ROI/Competitive advantage]

[Name]

On [time and place] you emphasised that [specific strategic goal] is critical for [business outcome] and that achieving this would give us [specific competitive advantage/financial impact].

But I'm concerned that our current budget allocation puts us [specific risk] behind [competitor/timeline], potentially costing us [quantified opportunity].

So I'd like to request [specific amount] to [specific solution].

This investment would [specific ROI/timeline] and position us to [strategic advantage].

I'll speak to your PA to find a time to discuss this before [relevant deadline]?

[appropriate salutation]

[Your name]

Your DNA challenge

This week, use the DNA structure for at least three important emails.

Track your results and ask yourself these questions.

- Was my response rate higher?
- Was the response time quicker?
- Was the quality of engagement better?
- Did people take action as a result?

The DNA structure isn't just another email technique - it's a fundamental shift in how you approach communication.

By starting with what matters to your reader you'll stop being seen as "just another sender" and turn into a trusted partner.

Now let's move on to the next chapter, where you'll discover the NAD structure for addressing urgent issues that demand immediate attention.

ENDNOTES

1   Allegedly
2   If you don't have it, find it.
3   If these references mean nothing we are happy to give details ... and we feel very old!
4   So, make our templates your own. Don't treat them as scripts.

THE "NAD" STRUCTURE - WHERE URGENCY MEETS CLARITY

When time is of the essence

Picture the scene.

It's 5:17pm on Friday. Any minute now you'll close your laptop and put your feet up for the weekend.

Tonight you sign off on the project that has caused more sleepless nights than that time you decided it was a good idea to binge the "Evil Dead" series.

Then the call comes.

Ryan has found a critical flaw that could derail the Monday morning launch.

You need to sort this out now and get everyone aligned tonight.

Never fear, NAD is here.

The NAD structure (Nightmare-Action-Dream) is your weapon of choice in any of the following situations.

- There's a real crisis that needs a swift decision
- You've found a problem that will only get worse with time
- You need to show decisive leadership under pressure
- You don't have time for an email tango

Unlike DNA, which eases people into your thinking, NAD grabs them by the lapels and says, "Let's talk. NOW!"

This is how it works.

The anatomy of an NAD email

NAD flips the traditional structure on its head by leading with the problem. Then it outlines the actions that will lead to a constructive outcome.

It's like running into a room and shouting, "The building's on fire. Grab that bucket of water. You'll thank me later."

It goes like this.

1. NIGHTMARE section (30-50 words)

Start with a clear, data-driven outline of the problem. Don't beat around the bush. Don't ease in gently. Whack them straight between the eyes ... up to a point

Your goal: To create appropriate urgency without causing panic.

Key elements:

- Lead with facts and data, not your opinion
- Show how this will have an effect on the business
- Keep your emotions controlled. Aim for "Houston, we have a problem." Not, "We're all going to die."

2. ACTION section (40-60 words)

Restore order and get straight to the point about a) what is being done, or b) what needs to be done.

There are many words that would work here. "HOWEVER" "SO" "CONSEQUENTLY" "AS A RESULT".

You could even use "BUT" ... in a much more positive sense.[1]

Your goal: To show that you're a problem solver and have a steady hand on this..

Key elements:

- Be specific about the actions you've already taken or need others to take
- Show your ownership and leadership of the situation
- Be crystal clear about timelines and the next steps

3. DREAM section (20-40 words)

Connect your actions to positive outcomes with phrases that show future focus. e.g."These steps will guarantee ..."

Your goal: To restore confidence and show that the crisis is manageable if everyone pulls together.

Key elements:

- Paint the picture of a successful outcome
- Connect to business objectives
- Give realistic timelines
- End with confident assurance, not false promises

NAD in action: before and after

Let's see how NAD can change crisis communication from an utterly ignorable mess to a totally focussed solution.

Before:

Subject: Project updates and some concerns that have come to my attention - please review

Hi team,

I wanted to reach out to touch base about one or two areas regarding the Johnson project, which as you know has been one of our key strategic initiatives this quarter. A few things have come to my attention about where we stand with the overall timeline and deliverables, and it would be great if we could sort them out sooner rather than later.

It seems like there might be some potential challenges with certain technical aspects of the project that could possibly impact our ability to meet the milestones we've been working toward. Specifically, there may be some integration issues with the API components that we've been developing.

I realise Friday night isn't ideal timing but I need to flag this as there might be one or two penalty clauses that could come into play.

Could we explore some alternative approaches or workarounds that might help us navigate these technical hurdles? I think we have it in us to use our collective expertise and problem-solving capabilities to find a path forward that works for everyone.

If anyone has any thoughts or suggestions about how we might address these challenges I'm available before close of play.

Thanks so much for your attention to this matter, and please don't hesitate to reach out.

Best regards,

Sarah

After:

Subject: Johnson API issue - recovery next steps 6pm

Team,

The Johnson Project has just failed quality testing because three critical endpoints returned error codes.

This puts Monday's launch at risk which would trigger the overrun penalty of £47,000.

But, I want to reassure you that I've taken the following steps.

- Lisa and Marcus are isolating the integration issues.
- I'm negotiating a 48-hour extension with the client.
- I've brought Alex on board because she sorted the Mitchell issue in 18 hours.

I need you all on Teams at 6pm for an Emergency Standup to let me know if I've missed anything.

With all of these steps we can fix this by Sunday evening and avoid the penalties.

Let's turn Monday's launch into Tuesday's champagne celebration!

REMEMBER: Emergency Standup on Teams at 6pm.

Sarah

What changed?

1. The subject line signaled a problem, a solution and a clear call to action
2. The nightmare section quantified the risk (£47,000 penalty) **IN BOLD**
3. The action section used "BUT" to signal a change in tone

4. But this time the tonal change was to the reassurance that immediate positive steps were being taken

5. The action items were short, sharp bullet points to make them scannable

6. This was followed by a specific call to action in bold (the 6pm Emergency Standup)

7. The dream section gave a realistic timeline

8. The call to action was repeated. **Remember: what gets repeated gets remembered.**

9. The tone was urgent but controlled - it was about leadership, not panic

How to craft your own NAD emails

Step 1: Assess the true urgency

Before using an NAD structure, ask yourself these questions.

- Is this genuinely important, or just important to me?
- Could it wait until tomorrow?
- Could I solve this with a less urgent approach?
- Is this the best channel for me to get attention?

Step 2: Put real numbers on the nightmare

Make the problem concrete and measurable.

- Sales are down 23% against target
- This server outage is costing us £12,000 a minute

- We're 5 days behind schedule on a 10-day project

Don't use vague disaster language like "this could be a catastrophe." Let your data do the talking. **Remember: big numbers pack an emotional punch.**

Step 3: Show immediate action

Don't just highlight problems. Solve them, show the way or ask for help.

- I've already called our backup supplier.
- The emergency response team is on site.
- I've rescheduled the client meeting to buy us 48 hours.
- I need three ideas from everyone in the next 30-minutes.
- I've put a meeting in for 3pm to get everyone's input.[2]

Step 4: Paint the picture of recovery

End with realistic hope and optimism

- Get this right and we'll beat the target for next quarter.
- The client has already emailed to say thank you for what we're doing.
- This might feel huge but it's an opportunity to streamline our entire process.

NAD email templates for crisis scenarios

Project crisis recovery

Subject: [Project Name] [issue] - recovery meeting [day/time]

Team,

[Project Name] is currently [specific delay/issue with data] against our [deadline/target], potentially [specific business consequence with numbers].

However, we've started a plan.

1. [Specific action]
2. [Specific action]
3. [Specific action and what you need from them]

[Key person] is leading the technical recovery while I manage client communications.

With this in place we'll [specific recovery outcome] by [realistic timeline] while [additional benefit or learning].

I need everyone at an emergency review meeting [specific time and place].

[Your name]

Customer issue escalation

Subject: [Client/Service] issue - response plan activated

Hi [Name],

We've received reports that [specific customer issue with impact data]. This affects [number] customers and could [specific business risk].

But I want to assure you that I've activated our incident response plan.

- [Specific team/person] is leading the technical fix, and
- [Specific person] is managing customer communications.

I expect an initial resolution by [timeframe].

With all this in place we'll have full service back on line by [specific time] and [specific improvement] will stop any recurrence.

Ultimately this will strengthen our relationships with [customer name].

I'll update you every [frequency] until it's resolved.

[Your name]

Budget/Resource crisis

Subject: Q3 budget overage - cost controls implemented

Hi [Name],

Our Q3 expenses are [percentage] over budget because of [specific cause]. This puts us [amount] over our approved allocation with [time period] remaining in the quarter.

As a result I've put some immediate cost controls in place.

- [Specific measure 1]
- [Specific measure 2]

And I've prioritised [essential activities].

This should reduce our overage to [lower amount] by [date].

All this means that we'll [key business specific outcome] and [another benefit … preferably personal to the reader].

I'm available at [time] if you need more information.

[Your name]

Pro tips for effective crisis communication

Use data to raise the stakes

Numbers make problems real and important.[3]

- Response time is up to 4.7 seconds vs. our 2-second target
- We're £125,000 over budget with 6 weeks remaining
- Customer satisfaction dropped 18 points in the last week

Show leadership under pressure

Use words that convey your commitment and control.

- **Don't Say**: It's not clear what we're going to do
- **Do Say**: I've put the emergency protocols in place
- **Don't Say**: Steps are being taken
- **Do Say**: The technical team is isolating the root cause

Make your call to action crystal clear

Kill any confusion by being specific.

- **Vague**: We need to discuss this urgently
- **Clear**: There's an emergency call at 3pm - dial-in details below
- **Vague**: Please respond ASAP
- **Clear**: I need your approval for the recovery plan by 5pm today

Follow up religiously

Crisis communication isn't one-and-done. Set your expectations for the next steps.

- I'll send updates every 2 hours until this is resolved
- The next status report is at 4pm regardless of progress
- I'll confirm the results before 17.30

When NAD goes wrong

Urgent situations need careful handling. Avoid these common NAD mistakes.

The boy who cried wolf

If you use NAD for a non-urgent situation you'll destroy your credibility faster than a politician's promise. Reserve it for a genuine crisis.

The blame game

NAD is about solving problems, not assigning blame.

- **Wrong**: Marketing screwed up the campaign launch.
- **Right**: The campaign metrics show 40% lower engagement.

The panic inducer

Urgency without a plan just spreads anxiety.

- **Wrong**: The servers are down and I don't know when they'll be back.

- **Right**: We've spotted severe server downtime. The technical team is on the backup protocols now.

The fake optimist
If you can't deliver it, don't promise it.

- **Wrong**: It will all be fine by tomorrow.
- **Right**: I'm expecting an initial recovery within 24 hours and full resolution by Friday.

The only way is up

Managing up with NAD: escalating crises to senior leadership

When you escalate a problem to senior leadership you need to demonstrate that you're managing the situation while keeping them in the loop about business-critical issues.

The key things you need to do with an **NAD** upward email are:

- Lead with any business impact and/or financial exposure
- Show the immediate actions that have already been taken
- Give them enough information to handle key stakeholders
- Provide clear escalation points if you need their support

Here is an example **NAD** template for handling a crisis.

Subject: [Project/Client] issue - [financial impact] exposure managed

[Name]

[Specific issue] has occurred on [project/client]. This creates [specific business risk] with potential exposure of [financial/reputational impact].

[Relevant stakeholder] will likely hear about this by [timeframe].

So, the following things are in place.

- We've activated our response plan: [specific actions taken].
- I'm personally managing [critical element]
- [Team members] are handling [other elements].

The current recovery timeline is [specific timeframe] with [success metric].

This positions us to [positive outcome] by [timeline] and will reassure [stakeholder] about our crisis management capabilities].

I'll update you at [specific interval] unless you need anything sooner. I'll also let you know if anything needs your immediate input.

[Your name]

Your NAD challenge

Obviously we hope this doesn't happen.

But if during the course of the next seven days "La merde frappe le ventilateur"[4] craft an NAD email and notice the following things.

- How quickly did you get responses?
- What was the quality of engagement from the recipients?
- Did people take immediate action?
- How was your leadership perceived under pressure?

And remember this: NAD is a power tool.

Use it wisely and people will trust your judgment and problem-solving leadership when you say something's urgent.

Overuse it and they'll start ignoring your real emergencies.

Next up: The AND structure for demonstrating proactivity and building collaborative partnerships.

ENDNOTES

1   In The DNA of Engagement® we talked about how "but" kicks the dream in the butt. We were going to call this more positive usage the "but-lift" but we're glad we didn't.

2   This is such an important thing to remember. If you see a problem and don't have the solution don't remain silent. Sometimes having the plan of how you will get help is enough.

3   In fact, data is so important as a persuasion tool that you should always make time to collect the key metrics.

4   Not actual French. If you find yourself in a Parisian pickle try,'Ça va barder'.

THE "AND" STRUCTURE - THE ART OF COLLABORATIVE LEADERSHIP

When the problems stack up you need to be the solution

Read this and try not to wince.

It's Friday afternoon and you're three weeks into leading a project with more moving parts than a Swiss watch.

The eyes of the leadership team are firmly trained on a successful delivery that will revolutionise how the company is viewed by its customers.

You think everything has been going smoothly until ... the perfect storm breaks.

In the space of an hour your inbox is flooded with emails from marketing who want segmentation heaven, sales who want lead-scoring nirvana and IT who want everyone to stop asking for "just one more field" in the database.

Suddenly you've gone from being the conductor of a symphony orchestra to a fire fighter putting out the flames of miscommunication.

What should you do?

Rattle off a bullet-pointed diatribe of each department's failures? Point and shout that, "If this doesn't get sorted out then heads will roll"?

Don't do either of those things.

What will save the day is if you can find a path to get everyone back on track and working towards the shared goal you always dreamed was possible.

A path that will lead to you becoming the corporate equivalent of Nick Fury in The Avengers as you bring remarkable individuals together to overcome extraordinary challenges.

You're about to discover that path: the AND structure..

The AND structure (Action - Nightmare - Dream) helps you do these things.

- Build collaboration based on the recognition of contribution
- Get the buy-in you need to take the project to the next stage
- Demonstrate proactive leadership

AND will transform you from a problem-causing zero to a solution-making hero who gets things done.

The anatomy of an AND email

The AND structure is well aware that it is facing a problem.

But it knows the problem involves egos and the only solution is to get those egos flying in formation.

AND is like the football[1] manager's talk just before extra-time when a great win is close but victory will rely on highly paid superstars putting their individual goals aside for the good of the team.

AND is a brilliant combination of EQ and IQ.

Let's look at how it works.

1. ACTION section (40-60 words)

You start by letting everyone know exactly what great work has been done so far and what it has meant. Be genuine and generous with your words. This is the old "praise in public" move.

Your goal: To make everyone feel seen and appreciated.

Key elements:

- Be specific about the actions that everyone has taken
- Include some positive numbers if you can

2. NIGHTMARE section (30-50 words)

Let everyone know that their great work could be for nothing if things don't change. The team could become their own nightmare without a collaborative mindset.

Your goal: To create a shared understanding that this is a big challenge which needs a combined effort if success is going to be guaranteed.

Key elements:

- Use "BUT" to get into the nightmare
- Frame the challenge as something that everyone owns
- Be honest about the difficulties and avoid melodrama

3. DREAM section (30-50 words plus call to action)

Connect to a future of collaborative success and the collective benefits.

Your Goal: To unite everyone in a journey towards mutual success and motivate them to collaborate.

Key elements:

- Emphasise the shared wins and mutual benefits
- Show everyone how they will be part of broader business objectives
- Show how teamwork will multiply any individual efforts
- End with a call to collaboration

AND in action: before and after

Let's change a "we've got a problem and the problem is you" email into a "you're doing amazing work that will get us home safely … if we all work together" message.

Before:

Subject: Multiple departmental failures that are going to need immediate intervention from everyone. URGENT!!!!

Team,

I need to address the significant performance issues that have become apparent across the customer data project. It's clear that several departments are failing to meet basic project requirements.

Marketing is consistently moving the goalposts and changing specifications without proper consultation, creating unnecessary work for other teams. This lack of strategic thinking is causing project delays and budget overruns.

IT continues to reject reasonable requests by claiming technical limitations, which suggests either inadequate planning or insufficient technical capabilities to deliver what was promised during the initial scoping phase.

Sales has been largely absent from critical discussions and appears to be operating independently without regard for project dependencies.

The cumulative effect of these departmental failures is that we're now significantly behind schedule and at risk of missing our deliverables. This is unacceptable.

Immediate improvement in cross-departmental coordination and accountability needs to be implemented NOW! Each team lead should prepare a detailed explanation of their current blockers and proposed solutions.

Going forward, all specification changes must be approved through proper channels, and I expect realistic timelines from IT rather than blanket rejections.

Meeting scheduled for tomorrow 9am sharp. Attendance is mandatory.

Sarah

After:

Subject: Customer project wins - final coordination Tuesday 8.30am

Hi everyone,

Congratulations on the work across the customer project so far.

- Marketing has transformed our customer understanding.
- IT is processing data 40% faster than before.

- Sales are smashing our conversion rates.

We're on the verge of something remarkable.

But in the final stages we need to avoid three potential traps.

1. Failing to understand how our efforts fit together
2. Making problems for each others' work streams
3. Missing key deadlines

Tackle these and we'll solve one of the CEO's biggest headaches while putting our team at the heart of the organisation's future.

I've put 45 minutes in everyone's diary at 8.30am on Tuesday to map out the final integration.

I'll bring coffee and a clear agenda so we can make the run in something to celebrate.

Best,
Sarah

What changed?

1. The subject line celebrates progress and looks forward
2. ACTION section specifically calls out each team's contributions
3. NIGHTMARE section is short, sharp and clear about the fact that a lack of combined team ethos will be the problem if we're not careful

4. DREAM section says how success delivers benefits for the team and a higher purpose (the CEO)

5. The call to action is clear and supportive (coffee!), not just another meeting

6. The tone is appreciative, energised and builds collective pride

How to craft your own AND emails

Step 1: Put everyone's contributions in the spotlight

Before you write a word make sure you understand what each person or team has genuinely added to the process.

- What value have they delivered?
- What problems have they solved?
- What progress can you measure and point to in celebration?
- Who has gone above and beyond all expectations?

Remember: AND only works if you're genuinely appreciative of what others have done.

Step 2: Connect their good work to solving big problems

Your AND emails should remind everyone that their excellent work is solving important challenges:

- Connect current efforts to big concerns or strategic imperatives

- Show how their work addresses problems that affect the whole organisation
- Remind them why this work matters beyond just completing a project

Step 3: Paint the collective picture of victory

Show how everyone's effort combines to create something magnificent

- When marketing's insights meet the conversion expertise in sales
- The combination of technical skills and creative vision
- Together we're building something none of us could create alone

Step 4: Take leadership initiative

Make collaboration happen.

- Put meetings in diaries rather than asking when people are free
- Prepare specific support structures
- Show that you're handling the logistics so others can focus on their expertise

Now that you understand the key elements let's look at a few frameworks that you can adapt to tackle some common collaboration conundrums.

AND email templates for collaborative scenarios

Project progress and team rallying

Subject: [Project Name] excellence - final integration plan ready

Hi team,

The work on [Project Name] has been outstanding.

The [high level praise e.g. quality] means we're on the verge of [what success will mean].

- [Team A] has [specific achievement],
- [Team B] has [specific achievement], and
- [Team C] has [specific achievement].

This work directly addresses [specific organisational challenge/board concern/strategic imperative] that's been flagged up in [relevant context - board meetings/analyst reports/client feedback].

But as we tackle the final integration we need to make sure that we don't [specific things that could get in the way].

Get it right and our combined efforts will [specific organisational impact] while [specific benefit for each team involved].

Here's the plan.

- [Specific action]
- [Specific action]
- [Specific action]

Together we can all make sure this project [specific outcome].

Best,
[Your name]

Cross-departmental appreciation and coordination

Subject: Cross-departmental wins - final coordination plan ready

Hi [names],

Our work over the past [timeframe] is really getting noticed.

- [Department 1] has [specific achievement]
- [Department 2] has [specific achievement]
- [Department 3] has [specific achievement]

This is exactly what will deliver [metrics].

But we've hit the point where without careful coordination we won't get the result that we've all worked so hard for.

Here is the plan for getting this thing over the line.

- [Specifics on timeframe, meetings, logistics, support]
- [Specifics on timeframe, meetings, logistics, support]
- [Specifics on timeframe, meetings, logistics, support]

Together we'll connect everyone's excellent work and celebrate our success.

Best,
[Your name]

Volunteer/Committee coordination

Subject: [Initiative/event] incredible work - coordination plan ready

Hi everyone,

The effort you've all put into [initiative/event] has been incredible.

- [Person/team] has [specific contribution]
- [Person/team] has [specific achievement]
- [Person/team] has [specific accomplishment]

But we now face the challenge of having a lot of good ingredients and not enough time to turn them into the cake we want.

This worries me because without a great end product your individual efforts could go unrecognised.

Here is the plan to make sure we make sure that doesn't happen.

- [Step one]
- [Step two]
- [Step three]

If we follow this it will bring all of our efforts together and deliver [positive data point].

Looking forward to making all of this a reality with you.

[Your name]

Pro tips for appreciative leadership communication

Here's what you need to keep in mind as you take AND to the next level.

Be specific about contributions

Generic praise will feel hollow. Be specific in your recognition of good work.

- **Generic**: Everyone's doing great work
- **Specific**: Sarah's user research insights changed our entire approach
- **Generic**: The team is working hard
- **Specific**: The engineering team delivered three critical fixes ahead of schedule

Join the dots between the individuals and collective success

Help people see how their contribution has affected the bigger picture:

- Your financial analysis provided the foundation for the entire strategy
- The design work you did is what made the client presentation so compelling
- Your documentation allowed the other teams to integrate so smoothly

Make collaboration feel like an opportunity, not an obligation

Use language that positions working together as a chance to make individual actions even more valuable.

- This is our chance to show what this team can accomplish
- Let's bring all these ideas together and create something remarkable
- The final push is where everyone's expertise gets the opportunity to shine

Take ownership of the next steps

- **Weak**: Maybe we should find time to meet
- **Strong**: I've put 30 minutes in everyone's diary for Thursday

- **Weak**: We should probably coordinate better
- **Strong**: I'll handle the coordination so you can focus on the work you're doing

Connect their work to the big impact

- Reference leadership concerns, strategic priorities or competitive challenges
- Show how their collaboration goes way beyond mere project completion
- Link their teamwork to the reputation or positioning of the organisation
- Remind them that their work will get noticed at the top

End with energy and support

- Let's finish this project as strongly as we started it
- I'll handle the logistics so we can all focus on the creative work
- Bring your best ideas - this is where it all comes together

But even the most appreciative AND can backfire if you fall into these traps.

When AND goes wrong

Avoid these mistakes to make sure your AND emails land with full power.

False praise

Don't invent contributions if they don't exist. It's a sure fire way to kill trust in your judgement and leadership. And it will undermine the real achievements.

The impossible dream

It's great to create a "stretch goal" that gets everyone fired up.

But don't start promising outcomes that no amount of brilliant teamwork will deliver.

Gold stars for plastic performances

Don't treat mediocre work like an exceptional achievement. Again, people will see through you in the blink of an eye.

Remember: The key to AND success is a genuine connection to specifics.

The only way is up

Managing up with AND: Coordinating cross-functional success for senior visibility

When you use **AND** in an upward direction you position yourself as the orchestrator of cross-departmental excellence and make sure that senior leadership sees the collective impact.

The key to successful **AND** upward communication is to show how individual team contributions are combining to deliver strategic outcomes that matter at board level.

The key things you need to do with an **AND** upward email are:

- Highlight measurable progress across multiple departments
- Connect team achievements to strategic priorities
- Position yourself as the key coordinator, not just a reporter
- Make it clear that continued success requires senior support/visibility

Here is an example **AND** template for making senior leadership aware of how cross-functional teams are coordinating to deliver their vision.

```
Subject: [Strategic initiative] on track -
final coordination [date]

[Name]

The work on [strategic initiative] you put in
place to address [specific challenge] has been
excellent.

    • [Department] has [specific achievement
      with metric]
    • [Department] has [specific achievement
      with metric]
    • [Department] has [specific achievement
      with metric].

But as we move into final integration we need to
avoid the problem of individual work streams
losing sight of the big picture.

I've scheduled a coordination session for
[timeframe] to make sure we hit [specific stra-
tegic outcome with data] by [date].

I'll update you on [date] and sooner if we
need your input.

Best,
[Your name]
```

This template positions you as someone who can see the big picture, coordinate excellence across silos and deliver strategic value - exactly the kind of leadership senior executives want to see developing in their organisation.

Your AND challenge

This week, find one situation where good work is happening in pockets but would be even better if it was coordinated.

As you craft your AND email make sure you do these things:

- Genuinely recognise specific contributions from different people
- Paint a picture of collective success
- Make collaboration feel like an opportunity to build on existing excellence

Then track how people respond.

- Did you feel that people felt more motivated to contribute?
- Did the teams coordinate more effectively?
- Did the quality of collaboration improve?

Remember: AND works because you're reminding people that they've started to build something great and you're inviting them to complete it.

The AND structure transforms you from a project manager into a collaboration catalyst.

And in a world full of people who highlight what's wrong, you'll be the leader who amplifies what's right and then gets things done.

Next up: The NDA structure for when the only option is to make significant change and transformation.

ENDNOTES

1   Soccer, if you must.

THE "NDA" STRUCTURE - FOR WHEN THE GOING GETS TOUGH

Sometimes tough love is the kindest option

WARNING! The following scenario could result in a blood pressure spike.

Monday morning. 9am. The powers that be are expecting final delivery of the project you've been leading by the end of business on Thursday.

It's crunch time.

You look at the project dashboard and progress is so slow that a wounded tortoise would speed past in the outside lane.

Then there are the rumblings from some line managers that they are seeing corners being cut on the "key deliverables"[1].

You've gone through the options that you read about in "The Art of the Unignorable Email".

You've inspired them with DNA emails. You've united them with AND.

And everyone's been terribly polite and promised to "circle back", "touch base" and "drill down into the issues".

But nothing's changed.

How's your blood pressure doing?

Dear reader, you've reached that moment every leader dreads and every team needs.

It's time for some tough love.

This isn't about getting mean and throwing people under the bus.

It is about being honest and calling out the things that aren't working so they can be fixed.

Because sometimes the kindest thing you can do is tell the truth.

This is where the NDA structure comes in.

Enter the NDA dragon

The NDA (Nightmare-Dream-Action) is your inversion of choice when enough is enough.

It will help you:

- Constructively address poor performance

- Reset expectations without destroying morale
- Create urgency for change and show a clear path forward

NDA doesn't sugarcoat problems, it calls them out.

But it does it in a way that focuses on solutions rather than blame, and builds a bridge from "this isn't working" to "here's how we fix it".

NDA will supercharge your reputation as a leader who isn't afraid to make the tough calls that get things done.

The anatomy of an NDA email

NDA follows a firm but fair structure that acknowledges reality, paints a better future and demands action.

1. NIGHTMARE section (60-80 words)

Start with a clear statement about what's not working. Be specific about the problems, honest about the impact and direct about why this matters. This isn't about attacking people - it's about calling out the reality that everyone can see but no one dares to say.

Your goal: To create undeniable clarity about what needs to change.

Key elements:

- Be specific about what's failing or underperforming
- Include concrete examples or metrics where possible

- Connect the problems to real business impact
- Avoid personal attacks but don't shy away from tough truths

2. DREAM section (40-60 words)

This is where you pivot into "But it doesn't have to be like this". It's where you paint a picture of what excellence will look like and why it's achievable. It's where you show that you believe in the team's ability to turn things around.

Your goal: To shift from problem focus to solution focus while maintaining urgency.

Key elements:

- Use "But" as your bridge from nightmare to possibility
- Be specific about what good performance looks like
- Connect improved performance to meaningful outcomes
- Show confidence that change is possible

3. ACTION section (30-50 words plus specific next steps)

The key is to end with clear, concrete actions that will drive the change you need. No vague calls to "do better". You need specific commitments with specific timelines.

Your goal: To create accountability and immediate forward momentum.

Key elements:

- Specific actions with specific deadlines
- Clear ownership of who does what
- Immediate next steps[2]
- Take ownership of facilitating the change

NDA in action: before and after

Let's transform a wishy-washy "we need to improve" message into a clear, constructive and compelling reset.

Before:

```
Subject: Touching base re: Wilson project. I've
got some thoughts to share when everyone has a
moment

Hi lovely team,

I hope you're all well and not feeling too over-
whelmed with everything that's been going on! I
know it's been a busy time for everyone and I
really appreciate all the hours you've been put-
ting in.

I've been doing some reflecting on the Wilson
account project and I wanted to share some obser-
vations that have been on my mind.

It seems like we might be experiencing some bumps
along the way with certain aspects of the project.
```

Nothing is wrong, per se, but there might be room for some improvements here and there. I know these things happen in any project and it's totally understandable given how complex everything has become.

I've had one or two messages from the client and they've shared some feedback that might be worth considering. They mentioned that some of our recent work could potentially benefit from a slightly different approach. I appreciate how hard everyone has been working but they are the client. Hey ho.

I think it would be wise if we explored some potential adjustments if that's OK.

With a bit of collaborative brainstorming and some fine-tuning I bet we'll figure out the best path forward in no time.

How is everyone fixed today or tomorrow?

Thanks in advance. I really appreciate you all.

Warmest regards,

Sarah

After:

Subject: Wilson Project Reset - new standards effective today

Morning team,

I need to be direct about the Wilson project.

- We've missed three consecutive deadlines
- Our last presentation had errors that the CMO caught before we did
- Recent analysis has been well below our usual standards

People are asking if we're the right partner and based on our current performance, it's a fair question.

But it doesn't have to be like this. Our work on Maygrove proves we have the talent to turn this around and show Wilson exactly why they chose us.

This is how we'll do it.

- All deliverables will be peer reviewed before submission.
- Daily check-ins at 8.45am will run until Thursday.
- There's a project reset meeting today at 2pm.

This is fixable if we commit to fixing it now.

Best,
Sarah

What changed?

- The language was sharper with direct short sentences.
- There were no euphemisms about "challenges" - just clear bullet points of what's going wrong.
- The consequences of the poor performance were crystal clear.
- After the honest and worrying opening there was the sharp pivot into "But it doesn't have to be like this" to create the bridge to solutions
- The actions were concrete and bullet pointed so there could be no excuse to miss them.
- It was all given a clear timeline.
- Sarah took ownership and made sure she showed faith in the team

How to craft your own NDA emails

Step 1: Get crystal clear on the problems

Before you write a word, make sure you're very clear on what's not working.

- What specific standards aren't being met?
- What is the measurable impact?
- How is this affecting the broader business or team?
- What will happen if this continues?

Remember: NDA only works if you're addressing real problems with real consequences.

Step 2: Paint the positive "But" picture

Your dream section needs to show that excellence is achievable.

- Reference past successes from this team
- Connect improved performance to meaningful outcomes
- Show that you believe change is possible

Step 3: Create immediate accountability

Make change happen now.

- Set specific review dates and check-in points
- Put new processes or standards in place
- Take ownership of driving the change

NDA email templates

Project performance reset

Subject: [Project Name] Performance Reset - new standards effective immediately.

Hi team,

I need to address where we stand on [Project Name].

- [Specific problems - missed deadlines, quality issues, client concerns].

This is having a real impact on [specific business consequences].

But it doesn't have to be like this. This team has delivered [specific past success] and has the expertise to [specific capability].

I have no doubt that we can turn this around and deliver [specific outcome].

Effective immediately,

- [specific new process/standard/accountability measure]
- [specific new process/standard/accountability measure]
- [specific new process/standard/accountability measure]

We're going to fix this.

Best,
[Your name]

Team standards reset

Subject: Team standards reset - excellence starts Monday

Hi [team],

I need to be honest about our recent performance.

- [Specific examples of substandard work/feedback from client].

This isn't the quality we're known for, and it's not fair to our clients or to each other to accept this as the new normal.

I know we're better than this. We've proven it with [specific past achievements] and we have the talent to [specific capability]. It's time to get back to the work that has made this team a success.

Starting Monday this is what we'll do.

- [specific new standards/processes].

I'm scheduling [specific accountability measures] and want to meet with everyone individually this week to ensure we're aligned on expectations.

Let's show everyone what we're really capable of.

Best,
[Your name]

Pro tips for powerful NDA

Use concrete evidence, not opinions

Weak: The quality hasn't been great
Strong: Three client deliverables contained errors that we should have caught

Weak: We're behind schedule
Strong: We've missed our last four deadlines by an average of six days

Reference past success to show belief

Weak: I know you can do better
Strong: Your analysis of the Peterson data was exactly the insight we needed now

Make the "But" transition powerful and aspirational

Weak: However, we can improve
Strong: But it doesn't have to be like this. We have the talent to turn this around

Create immediate and urgent action

Weak: We should probably meet soon to discuss
Strong: I've blocked 45 minutes at 3pm Thursday to map out our recovery plan

End with confidence

Weak: Hopefully we can sort this out
Strong: This is fixable if we start now

When NDA goes wrong

Even well-intentioned tough love can backfire if you fall into these traps.

The personal attack in public

Wrong: John's attitude is dragging down the whole team
Right: Our error rate has doubled over the past month and is affecting client confidence

Focus on performance and impact, not personality or character.

Impossibly high standards

Wrong: From now on, everything must be perfect
Right: All client deliverables require peer review before submission

Set challenging but achievable standards with clear processes.

The threat without support

Wrong: Shape up or ship out
Right: I'm putting daily checks in place to help us get back on track

Combine accountability with support and clear next steps.

The vague nightmare

Wrong: Things haven't been going well
Right: We've missed three deadlines and received formal client complaints

Be specific about problems so people can address them specifically.

Your NDA challenge

This week, identify one area where performance genuinely isn't meeting standards and tough love is needed.

Before you send your NDA email:

- Document the specific problems with specific evidence
- Identify past successes that prove capability
- Create concrete actions with clear timelines
- Schedule the follow-up meeting

Then track the results:

- Did performance improve immediately?
- Did team members step up to the challenge?

- Was the tough conversation actually appreciated?
- Did setting clear standards create better outcomes?

Remember: NDA isn't about being harsh. It's about being honest enough to say that "enough is enough" and demand the excellence that your team is capable of delivering.

The balance between AND and NDA

The trick to being a smart leader is knowing when to use which structure.

Use AND when: Good work exists but needs coordination and collaboration
Use NDA when: Performance is genuinely substandard and needs a reset

Both structures respect your team enough to tell the truth.

- AND celebrates the things that are working and builds on them
- NDA highlights what isn't working and shows the path to fix it

Your choice isn't between being the nice leader or the tough leader.

Your choice is to be the effective leader who gets the best out of their team by giving them exactly what they need, when they need it.

Sometimes that's appreciation and collaboration. Sometimes it's accountability and challenge.

The truly great leaders know the difference.

Next up: The ROAD structure for when you need to deliver difficult messages that no one wants to hear but everyone needs to understand and accept.

ENDNOTES

1   When will these people ever be specific?
2   And yes , an immediate all hands review meeting counts.

THE "ROAD" STRUCTURE - WHEN YOU CAN'T AVOID THE DIFFICULT PATH

The road you hope you never have to travel

Picture the scene.

It's 6.30am. You wake up and fumble for your phone.

Dear God! WhatsApp looks like it's been at an all night rave. What on earth is happening.

Two minutes later you've got a pretty good idea.

The numbers are brutal. The market has shifted. And the board has made decisions that make root canal work sound like a long weekend in Mallorca.

Within the next hour you are going to have to deliver news up, down and across that could make everyone's day feel significantly worse.

What do you do?

- You can't DNA your way out of it with rapport-building.
- You can't NAD it because it's not a crisis that can be solved.
- You can't AND it because there's no brilliant work to celebrate.
- And you definitely can't NDA it because this isn't about performance.

This is about harsh realities beyond anyone's control that they won't want to hear but absolutely must understand and accept.

Welcome to the road that we definitely hope is less travelled but is sometimes unavoidable.

Welcome to ROAD.

When you're forced onto the side road

The ROAD structure (Reality-Outcome-Acceptance-Direction) is your GPS when you need to deliver news that is:

- Necessary but unwelcome (budget cuts, layoffs, strategic pivots)

- Made above your level but is yours to implement
- Based on external factors that nobody can control
- Final and non-negotiable, no matter how people might feel about it

ROAD doesn't try to make people feel happy about bad news.

It helps them understand what is happening, why it's happening and what comes next. Delivered well it allows them to move forward productively and avoid getting stuck in denial or resentment.

Think of ROAD as the emergency service for an organisational car crash. It acknowledges the pain while focusing on survival and recovery.

The anatomy of a ROAD email

ROAD follows a direct but compassionate structure that explains the reality, states the decisions clearly, validates what people are feeling and focuses on constructive next steps.

1. REALITY section (40-60 words)

Start with the objective empirical facts that forced this decision. Don't give your opinion, don't lay any blame, just itemise the circumstances that made this choice inevitable.

Your goal: To help people understand that this wasn't arbitrary or avoidable.

Key elements:

- Lead with market conditions, financial data or external pressures
- Use specific numbers and concrete facts
- Avoid emotional language - stick to objective reality
- Show that these circumstances are beyond anyone's control

2. OUTCOME section (20-40 words)

Be very clear and direct about the decision. No euphemisms, no softening language, no beating around the bush.

Your goal: To create absolute clarity about what's happening.

Key elements:

- Use simple, direct language
- Avoid corporate speak and euphemisms
- Be specific about what's changing and when

3. ACCEPTANCE section (30-50 words)

Acknowledge that this is a difficult time while explaining why it's necessary. Your job isn't to make people feel better. It's to help them understand.

Your goal: To validate the emotions while reinforcing necessity.

Key elements:

- Acknowledge that this news is unwelcome
- Connect to organisational survival or long-term success
- Show that alternatives were genuinely considered[1]
- Be honest about the difficulty without dwelling on it

4. DIRECTION section (40-60 words)

Focus on moving forward constructively. This is about practical next steps, not motivation or inspiration.

Your goal: To channel everyone's energy toward productive action rather than unproductive resistance.

Key elements:

- Outline the immediate next steps with clear timelines
- Specify what support is available to everyone
- Be concrete about implementation
- End with a focus on future success, not current disappointment

ROAD in action: before and after

Let's stop shying away from "difficult news'" by turning it into clear, compassionate and direct communication.

Before:

```
Subject: Brief leadership update. There may be
some adjustments ahead
```

Dear team,

I'm reaching out with some updates from recent leadership discussions.

There's been some interesting conversations at ExCo about various market dynamics and organisational positioning. It seems like there might be some shifts happening across the industry that could potentially influence how we approach certain aspects of our strategy moving forward.

The leadership team has been exploring different scenarios and conducting planning exercises to ensure we're well-positioned for whatever the future might hold. As part of this forward-thinking process there have been some discussions about potential adjustments to our current operational framework.

Some of these adjustments might involve resource optimisation and strategic realignment in certain functions. This could impact various aspects of how we've been doing things.

I know change can feel unsettling and I want to assure everyone that these decisions haven't been made lightly.

I'm committed to keeping everyone informed as more details become available, and I'll be reaching out to schedule individual conversations with each of you to discuss how these organisational enhancements might affect your particular role and responsibilities.

In the meantime, please know that I have complete confidence that with collective resilience and positive attitudes we'll emerge from this adjust-ment period even stronger than before.

If anyone has any immediate concerns or questions about this preliminary communication please don't hesitate to reach out.

Looking forward to continuing our journey together.

With appreciation,

Sarah

After:

Subject: Q4 Budget Reduction - Immediate Changes Needed

Team,

The board just sent me the following news.

- Industry spending is down 31% this quarter
- Our three largest clients have cut budgets by 25% +

The downturn is affecting every agency. Two announced layoffs this week.

Here's how we're going to avoid that.

- We're reducing our Q4 operational budget by 35%
- We're pausing all new hires until January
- The December conference is cancelled

I know this will disrupt your plans but it will also help us keep the full team in place.

This is what's happening from tomorrow.

- We'll restructure the Q4 deliverables at a team meeting on Wednesday
- I'll schedule 1-1 meetings by Friday to set individual targets

None of us wanted this but together we will emerge stronger when market conditions improve.

Best,
Sarah

What changed?

1. The subject line is direct about what's happening
2. REALITY section uses specific data, not vague challenges
3. OUTCOME section states the decisions clearly without euphemisms
4. ACCEPTANCE section validates disappointment while explaining necessity
5. DIRECTION section provides concrete next steps with specific timelines

6. The tone is straightforward but not heartless

7. The focus shifts from the bad news to productive forward movement

8. Everything is bullet pointed to make it easy to scan

How to navigate your own side roads

Step 1: Document the driving forces

Before crafting your message, get crystal clear on the external factors.

- What market conditions, financial pressures or competitive threats are driving this?

- What specific data or circumstances made this decision unavoidable?

- What would happen if these decisions weren't made?

- What alternatives were genuinely considered and why wouldn't they work?

Step 2: Strip away the corporate waffle

Be direct about what's happening:

- **Not**: We're rightsizing our human capital allocation

- **But**: We're cutting twelve positions across three departments

- **Not**: We're pivoting our go-to-market strategy

- **But**: We're stopping the direct sales approach and moving to online-only

Step 3: Validate feelings without wallowing

Acknowledge difficulty without becoming overly dramatic

- **Don't Say:** I know this is devastating
- **Do Say:** I know this is disappointing
- **Don't Say:** This destroys everything we've built
- **Do Say:** This affects the plans we've worked so hard to realise

Step 4: Make the way forward concrete

Give people specific ways to channel their energy productively:

- Schedule the meetings to look at implementation plans
- Give clear timelines for the transition
- Offer specific support resources
- Set expectations for how success will be measured

ROAD email templates for difficult decisions

Budget cut announcement

Subject: Budget cuts effective [date] - [Department/area] changes outlined

Team,

Unfortunately [specific external factors with concrete data] have created financial pressures that require immediate cost reductions.

Here's what you need to know.

- [Specific area and specific amount/percentage]
- [Specific area and specific amount/percentage]
- [Specific area and specific amount/percentage]

I understand this impacts [specific work/plans] in which you've invested considerable effort.

These cuts weren't made lightly but this approach best protects [specific outcomes] during [specific challenging period].

I'll be available on [your availability for communication] for [specific support].

We're focusing on [specific priorities] that will position us for [specific future success].

Best,
[Your name]

Strategic pivot announcement

Subject: Strategic pivot - [new approach] effective [date]

Hi [team/stakeholders],

I'm sorry to report that [specific market conditions/competitive pressures/customer feedback with data] show that our current approach to [specific area] is no longer viable.

From [date], we're shifting from [old approach] to [new approach], which means [specific operational changes].

I recognise these changes will [impact the changes will have on the recipients].

Here's what is happening right away.

- [Specific implementation steps with timeline]
- [Specific implementation steps with timeline]
- [Specific implementation steps with timeline]

This pivot will position us to [specific future opportunity or outcome with metrics] rather than continuing down a path that the market conditions have made unsustainable.

Best,
[Your name]

Restructuring communication

Subject: Organisational restructure - changes effective [date]

Team,

[Business reasons, specific data] have made it an imperative that we reorganise how we operate.

As of [date], these changes will come into place.

- [specific structural changes, who will be affected and how]

- [specific structural changes, who will be affected and how]
- [specific structural changes, who will be affected and how]

I know changes can create uncertainty and disrupt the working relationships that we've all worked so hard to establish.

But this restructure will address [specific business need], enable [specific organisational capability] and position us for [specific future success].

Here are the key milestones you all need to know.

- [specific transition timeline, process, support]
- [specific transition timeline, process, support]
- [specific transition timeline, process, support]

I'm available for clarification meetings at [give your availability].

Best,
[Your name]

Pro tips for navigating bumpy roads

Lead with external reality, not internal decisions

Weak: The leadership team has decided to make some changes

Strong: Market conditions have deteriorated 28% this quarter, forcing cost reductions

Use concrete language, not corporate euphemisms

Weak: We're right-sizing our workforce composition

Strong: We're cutting fifteen positions in operations and marketing

Acknowledge impact without dwelling on pain

Weak: I know this is absolutely devastating news that will ruin your plans

Strong: I understand this affects the projects you've worked hard on

Focus on forward movement, not current disappointment

Weak: I hope somehow we can make the best of this awful situation

Strong: These tough decisions will put us in a position to emerge strongly when market conditions improve

When the ROAD gets rocky

Even well-intentioned difficult communication can result in a car crash if you make these mistakes.

The blame game

Wrong: Corporate forced this on us. I disagree but have to implement it

Right: Market pressures require cost reductions across all divisions

Take ownership of "driving the car" even when you didn't choose the route.

The false optimist

Wrong: This is actually a great opportunity for everyone
Right: This positions us for recovery when conditions improve

Don't pretend bad news is good news, but do connect to future stability.

The doom spiral

Wrong: This is terrible. Everything is falling apart and it might get worse
Right: These are difficult but necessary changes that will address current market conditions

Be honest about difficulty without creating despair.

The vague direction

Wrong: We'll figure something out and get back to you
Right: I'm scheduling individual meetings Wednesday, Thursday and Friday to address how this will affect you specifically

Give concrete next steps, not vague promises to "circle back".

With all this in mind here's how you can get ROAD worthy with senior leadership.

The only way is up

Managing up with ROAD: Delivering bad news to senior leadership

Senior leaders need bad news delivered with context, options and clear recommendations for moving forward.

The key differences for managing up are:

- Start with any external factors they'll need to explain to others
- Show that you understand the wider business implications
- Present options with your recommendations
- Give them the narrative they'll need for stakeholders

Here is a ROAD template for upward delivery of bad news.

```
Subject: [Project] [impact] - external fac-
tors require decision

[Name]

[External factor with specific data] has cre-
ated [impact] on [project].

This affects our [business impact] and puts
[business goal] at risk.
```

```
I appreciate this could [potential impact for
recipient].

We have evaluated all avenues for next steps
and here are the recommended options.

  ● [specific option] to [business rationale]
  ● [specific option] to [business rationale]
  ● [specific option] to [business rationale]

This will allow us to [specific benefit] while
minimising [specific risk].

I can have a detailed recovery plan for you
by [timeframe] and handle the [value you can
add] if you prefer.

[Your name]
```

Your ROAD challenge

Hopefully you'll never need to use ROAD.

But if circumstances force you off your ideal route here's what we want you to do.

Before sending your ROAD email:

- Document the external factors that drove the decision
- Prepare specific next steps with clear timelines
- Practise delivering the news without emotional language

- Schedule the follow-up meetings to address implementation

After delivery make sure you track:

- How quickly people moved from shock to acceptance
- Whether implementation went smoothly or with resistance
- If your direct communication built or damaged trust
- Whether focusing on direction helped people to stop dwelling on disappointment

Remember: ROAD isn't about making people happy about bad news. It's about helping them understand, accept and move forward when the circumstances call for difficult changes.

ENDNOTES

1   If this is true

AND SO, WE ARRIVE AT THE BEGINNING

Your email evolution starts here

When David was studying screenwriting as part of his degree he spent three days locked in a central London lecture theatre with about 200 fellow students and the sadly departed Hollywood script legend Blake Snyder.[1]

As they came to the last minutes of what had been an intense period of watching and deconstructing classic movies scene by scene Snyder said to them all, "And so, we arrive at the beginning. You've got all the knowledge. It's now down to you to go out there as writers and put it into action."

You too, dear reader, have arrived at the beginning. You have all the knowledge you need to be a superhero of the sent box. All you need to do now is accept the challenge and put it to work.

Let's help you do that by sending you off with a final DNA inversion - the ADN (Action - Dream - Nightmare) because ... well we can, and we should practice what we preach with this incredibly versatile framework.[2]

Here goes.

Action - Look what you've built

While you've been reading this book something extraordinary has happened.

You've evolved from someone who crossed your fingers and hoped your emails worked, into someone who engineers them with precision and knows that they will be the difference that makes the difference.

You now have a complete leadership communication system that you can deploy with ease at exactly the right moment.

- **DNA** for building trust and rapport with sceptical stakeholders
- **NAD** for managing crises with clarity and decisive leadership
- **AND** for rallying collaboration and coordinating excellence

- **NDA** for driving accountability and demanding performance
- **ROAD** for delivering difficult truths with dignity and direction

You've mastered the art of creating emails that don't just get read - they get results.

Dream - The leader you've become

This positions you as the leader that others follow.

Not because of your title but because you can translate vision into action with your precise communication.

Every email you send demonstrates your ability to think strategically, lead under pressure and drive results.

You have three tools of competitive advantage at your fingertips.

1. **Speed**: The frameworks give you a quick path to successful communication
2. **Credibility**: Your emails show your leadership before you even enter the room
3. **Influence**: Your ideas now have the psychological strength to land and stick

And in a world where it is increasingly difficult to get people to pay attention and keep paying it you now hold the keys to the bank.

Nightmare - What you've escaped

Without these frameworks you wouldn't have the five key qualities of great leadership communication.

1. Relevance
2. Clarity
3. Action orientation
4. Emotional resonance
5. Strategic structure

And you'd still be trapped in a cycle of wrestling your words into life before sending them into a digital jungle to die without trace.

Which leaves you with a simple binary choice.

Your moment of choice

Our clients keep telling us that The DNA of Engagement® may well be the only communication approach that any business person will ever need.

But the DNA is just a framework. And frameworks are only as good as the people who apply them.

So this is your choice.

1. Do I keep doing what I've always done?
2. Do I use this framework to define the next phase of my career?

Before you answer, consider this.

If your emails improved by 10%, how much would that change your visibility, your reputation and your influence? Now multiply that number across the whole team that you lead.

The choice is simple isn't it.

I human take thee AI

Before we finish our journey we need to have a chat about you and AI.

Whether we like it or not, the bots are here to stay.

Every day they are getting better at filtering the dross from your inbox and they are getting smarter at composing personalised and efficient emails that follow impeccable grammar rules and keep a professional tone.

As a thought leader of the future you need to enter into a marriage of equals where you add your human heart to the power of AI.

Of course AI is a technical revolution.

But it is the same as any revolution that has eliminated routine work and allowed humans to elevate their uniquely human skills.

The printing press didn't kill storytelling - it made great storytellers more valuable. The calculator didn't eliminate mathematicians - it freed them to solve bigger problems.

See AI in a similar vein.

Let Gemini, Copilot, Apple Intelligence and many more handle the grammar, structure and basic responses while you add the things that only you can provide.

- Empathy
- Genuine understanding
- True connection to another person's experience.

Embrace the technology by using the prompts we will give you. Then refine its output with the EQ you have discovered in "The Art of the Unignorable Email".

Combine these two things and we guarantee that you'll stand out from everyone who hands over total control to the AI overlords.

All that will be left for you to do is pass on the tips that will let humans surf the inexorable wave of artificial intelligence, add their own flips and twists and arrive on shore as unignorable winners.

ENDNOTES

1   Google his seminal book on screenwriting and storycraft, "Save the Cat".
2   There will be bonus prizes for people who craft an ADN email

AI PROMPTS FOR DNA FRAMEWORKS

And now we come to that promised marriage between the humanity of your EQ and the heavy lifting muscle of AI.

We'll give you a couple of prompts now so you can get going immediately and you can download the rest with your bonus extras.

See these prompts as the start of a conversation between you and ChatGPT, Claude, Gemini or your email platform's AI assistant.

Let them give you the skeleton while you add the soul.

We're going to start with how to create great subject lines.

Universal subject line prompt

Since the subject line is that all important gateway to everything else in your email add these requirements immediately after the context element in every prompt you use.

You'll see how to do this in the DNA prompts that follow.

This will let the AI know that it needs to write a subject line that grabs attention and craft an email that delivers on that promise.

Subject line requirements:

- Communication direction: [Up/Down/Across]
- 6-10 words maximum
- Front-load the most important information in first 25 characters
- Include specific personalisation (name/department/project/deadline)
- Match the style to the communication direction:
  - **Upward**: Strategic impact, results or risks
  - **Downward**: Clarity, action, and support
  - **Across**: Collaboration, shared goals, mutual benefits
- Avoid: ALL CAPS, excessive punctuation, vague terms like "update' or "touching base"

Remember: Apply The Monday Morning Test before you send any email.

Would someone scanning 47 emails on their phone while distracted open yours immediately?

DNA prompts: building rapport and trust

Basic DNA prompt
Context:

- Recipient: [Name and role]
- My relationship with them: [New/uncertain/need to rebuild trust]
- What they care about: [Their priority/goal]
- The challenge: [Specific obstacle]
- What I need: [Your request]
- Communication direction: [Up/Down/Across]

Subject line requirements: [Paste the universal subject line requirements here]

Since this is DNA (building rapport), focus on the benefit to THEM:

- Examples: "Opportunity to [their goal]" or "[Their priority] - input needed"
- Avoid generic phrases like "Following up" or "Quick question"

Email structure:

- DREAM (25-40 words): Connect to what matters to the recipient

- NIGHTMARE (15-30 words): Introduce a relevant challenge with "BUT"
- ACTION (25-40 words): Propose collaborative solution with "THEREFORE/SO"

Write a professional email following this structure. Keep it under 150 words total.

Advanced DNA prompt
Recipient profile:

- Name: [Name]
- Role: [Job title]
- Recent conversation/context: [Specific reference]
- Their stated priority: [What they said matters to them]
- Communication style: [Formal/casual/data-driven/relationship-focused]
- Communication direction: [Up/Down/Across]

Email purpose:

- My goal: [What you want to achieve]
- Specific request: [What you need them to do]
- Deadline/urgency: [Timeline]

Subject line requirements: [Paste the universal subject line requirements here]

Since this is DNA (building rapport), focus on benefit to recipient:

- Include specific reference to their priority or recent conversation

- Examples: "[Their goal] acceleration opportunity" or "[Referenced project] - next steps ready"

Email structure:

- DREAM: Reference their specific priority and use "AND" to link to future benefits
- NIGHTMARE: Use "BUT" + specific data/example showing risk to their priority
- ACTION: Use "THEREFORE/SO" + collaborative language + clear call to action

The subject line should be under 50 characters and value-focused.

Subject line testing prompt

Use this prompt to improve any subject line:

Context:

- Email type: [DNA/NAD/AND/NDA/ROAD]
- Recipient: [Role/relationship]
- Communication direction: [Up/Down/Across]
- Main request/message: [What you want them to do]

Apply these criteria:

- The Monday Morning Test: Would someone scanning 47 emails while distracted open this?
- 25-character rule: Is the key information in the first 25 characters?
- Word count: Is it 6-10 words?

- Personalisation: Does it include relevant, specific information?
- Direction alignment: Does it match up/down/across communication needs?

PROVIDE:

- Analysis of current subject line's weaknesses
- 3 improved alternatives
- Explanation of why each improvement works better

How to customise your prompts

Industry-specific additions:

- Add relevant terminology and metrics for your field
- Include compliance or regulatory considerations
- Reference industry-standard processes or benchmarks

Communication style adjustments:

- Formal organisations: Add more structured language, titles, protocols
- Startup environments: Use a more casual tone, faster decision-making language
- Technical teams: Include specific technical details and metrics
- Creative teams: Allow for more expressive language and storytelling

Relationship modifications:

- New relationships: Emphasise credibility-building and clear explanations

- Established relationships: Reference shared history and use shorthand
- Senior stakeholders: Focus on strategic impact and bottom-line results
- Peer communications: Emphasise mutual benefit and collaboration

Improving your prompts over time

Track what works:

- Save prompts that generate particularly effective emails
- Note which elements get the best responses from recipients
- Adjust word counts based on your communication preferences

Refine based on feedback:

- Ask recipients what resonates most in your emails
- Test different versions of key phrases or structures
- Adapt timing and urgency indicators to your organisation's culture

Build your prompt library:

- Create variations for different types of stakeholders
- Develop specialised versions for recurring situations
- Build templates for your most common communication challenges

Important reminders

Always add the human element:

- Specific personal references AI cannot know
- Strategic insight about timing and organisational dynamics
- Your authentic voice and communication style

Never let AI handle these things

- Confidential or sensitive information
- Complex interpersonal conflicts
- Nuanced organisational politics
- Final decision-making on important communications

Best practices:

- Always review and edit AI output before sending
- Test prompts with less critical emails first
- Keep refining based on response quality and feedback
- Use AI for structure, add humanity for connection

Remember: The future belongs to those who can harness AI's efficiency while amplifying their human insight. These prompts are your starting point - make them uniquely yours.

YOUR 5-MINUTE EMAIL AUDIT

Use this quality control checklist before sending any important internal email

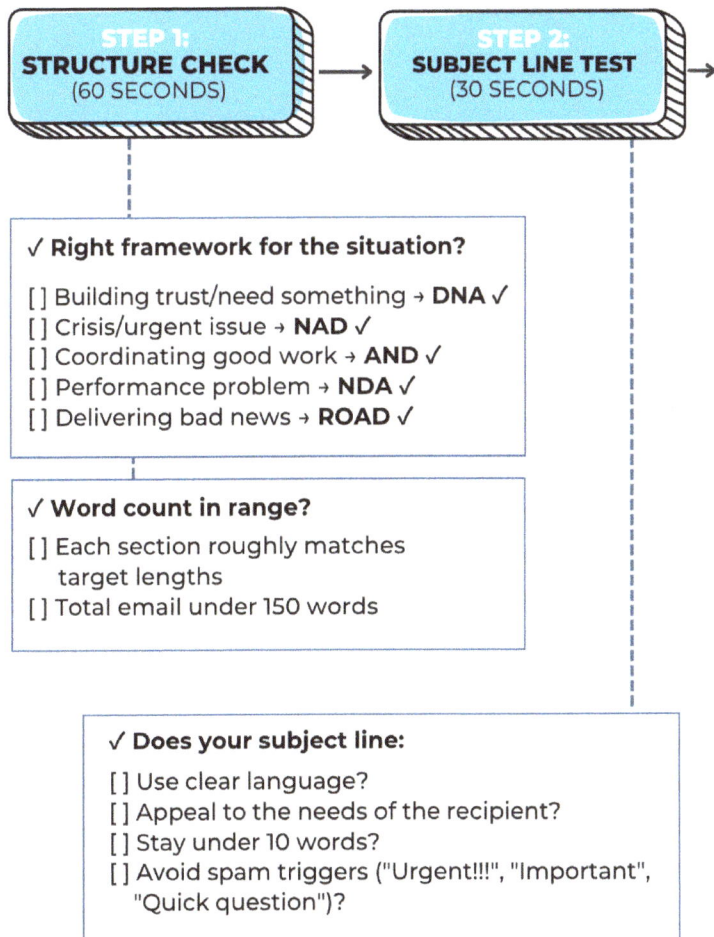

```
┌─────────────────┐       ┌─────────────────┐
│     STEP 1:      │  →    │     STEP 2:      │  →
│ STRUCTURE CHECK  │       │ SUBJECT LINE TEST│
│   (60 SECONDS)   │       │   (30 SECONDS)   │
└─────────────────┘       └─────────────────┘
```

✓ Right framework for the situation?

[ ] Building trust/need something → **DNA** ✓
[ ] Crisis/urgent issue → **NAD** ✓
[ ] Coordinating good work → **AND** ✓
[ ] Performance problem → **NDA** ✓
[ ] Delivering bad news → **ROAD** ✓

✓ Word count in range?

[ ] Each section roughly matches
   target lengths
[ ] Total email under 150 words

✓ Does your subject line:

[ ] Use clear language?
[ ] Appeal to the needs of the recipient?
[ ] Stay under 10 words?
[ ] Avoid spam triggers ("Urgent!!!", "Important",
   "Quick question")?

Quick fix: If you can't tell what action you want just from the subject line, rewrite it.

STEP 2.5:
DIRECTION AND
AUDIENCE CHECK
(30 SECONDS)

✓ **Upward communication specific:**

[] Does your email demonstrate strategic thinking (not just tactical requests)?
[] Have you connected your request to business priorities they care about?
[] Is the business impact/ROI clearly quantified where possible?
[] Is the email concise enough for senior leadership time constraints?
[] Does the subject line indicate clear business value (not just your need)?

✓ **Downward communication specific:**

[] Have you provided enough context for your team to understand the "why"?
[] Are expectations and next steps crystal clear?
[] Does the tone balance authority with collaboration?

✓ **Cross-functional communication specific:**

[] Have you acknowledged their priorities/constraints?
[] Is the mutual benefit clearly articulated?
[] Does the request feel collaborative rather than demanding?

⚙ **Quick direction fix:** If you are communicating up and your email feels too detailed or process-focused, cut the background information and lead with the business impact. If you are communicating down and it feels too terse, add more context about the "why".

STEP 3:
AI RESISTANCE SCAN
(60 SECONDS)

STEP 4:
CLARITY AND ACTION TEST
(90 SECONDS)

✓ **Personalisation check:**

[ ] References specific meeting/ conversation/context?
[ ] Uses the recipient's name?
[ ] Includes details only internal colleagues would know?
[ ] Avoids template language?

✓ **Scannability:**

[ ] Key information in first 50 words?
[ ] Important data in **bold** (sparingly)?
[ ] Call to action stands alone/is easy to spot?

✓ **Specificity check:**

[ ] Contains at least one concrete data point/metric?
[ ] Uses department/company- specific terminology?
[ ] Mentions specific people, projects or deadlines?

✓ **Mobile readability:**

[ ] Critical information visible without scrolling?
[ ] Sentences under 20 words where possible?
[ ] Bullet points used for multiple items?

✓ **Call to action quality:**

[ ] Specific request?
[ ] Clear deadline or timeframe?
[ ] Easy to respond to (multiple choice vs. open-ended)?
[ ] Assumes meeting will happen vs. asks if free?

STEP 5:
EMOTIONAL TONE
CHECK (60 SECONDS)

✓ Does the tone match your structure?

[ ] **DNA**: Collaborative and respectful ✓
[ ] **NAD**: Urgent but controlled ✓
[ ] **AND**: Appreciative and energising ✓
[ ] **NDA**: Direct but supportive ✓
[ ] **ROAD**: Honest but compassionate ✓

✓ Relationship check:

[ ] Appropriate level of formality for recipient?
[ ] Acknowledges their priorities/perspective?
[ ] Builds rather than damages relationships?

RED FLAG ALARM SYSTEM

STOP and rewrite if any of these apply:

[ ] You can't summarise your request in one sentence
[ ] The subject line could apply to any company/situation
[ ] There's no specific data, names or concrete details
[ ] The call to action is vague or missing
[ ] The tone feels off for the relationship/situation
[ ] The email addresses your needs without connecting
    to theirs
[ ] There's more than one main request[1]

The ultimate test questions

Before hitting send, honestly answer these questions.

1. "If I received this email I wouldn't know what to do
   and why it matters?"
2. "The recipient won't look good/smart when they
   respond?"
3. "This email could hurt my professional reputation?"

**If you scream "YES" to
any of these statements** ➡ **KEEP EDITING**

FINAL SEND DECISION

1 **Green Light** (All must be true):

[ ] Right structure for the situation
[ ] Clear and specific call to action
[ ] Contains personalised, internal context
[ ] Tone matches relationship and urgency
[ ] Will help recipient make a good decision

Send with confidence

2 **Yellow Light** (Fix before sending):

[ ] One or two criteria missed
[ ] Minor clarity or tone issues

Quick revision needed

3 **Red Light** (Major rewrite required):

[ ] Right structure for the situation
[ ] Clear and specific call to action
[ ] Contains personalised, internal context
[ ] Tone matches relationship and urgency
[ ] Will help recipient make a good decision

Stop. Start again with the diagnostic

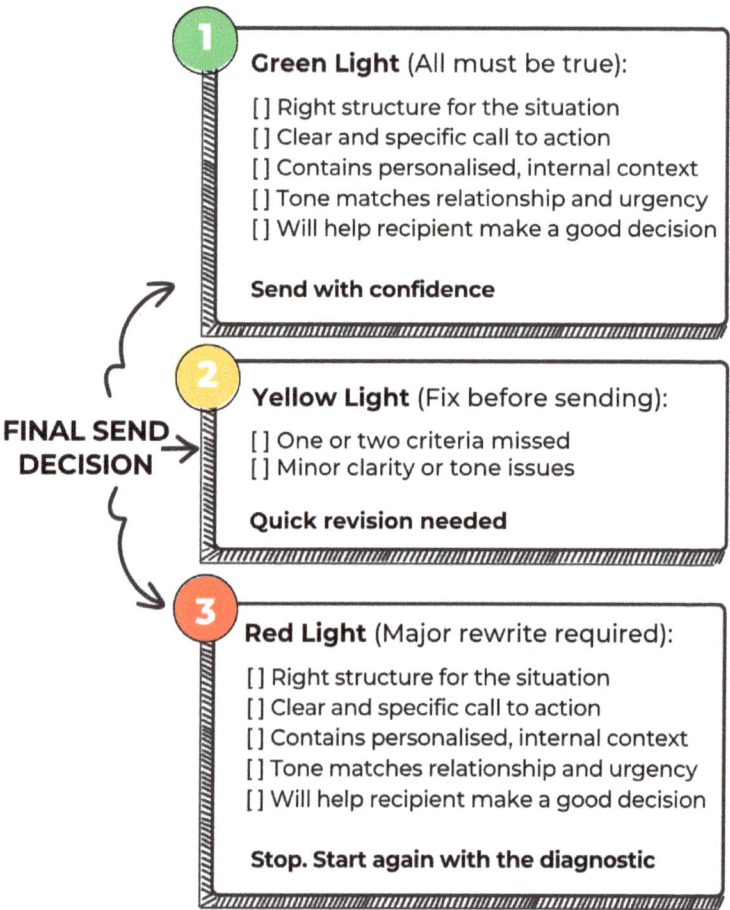

Remember: Five minutes of audit can save five days of follow-up emails.

ENDNOTES

1   Split these into separate emails

YOUR FREE STUFF

Head over to https://www.thednaofengagement.com/the-art-of-the-unignorable-email right now and sign up to get access to all the templates you've seen in this book and two bonus extras we've got waiting for you.

1. AI prompts for all of the DNA inversions
2. Free access to "The 'What Email' Advisor" app

"The 'What Email' Advisor" will help you make a quick decision about exactly what email you need to send in any given circumstances. It will also give you some coaching around how to add your EQ to the AI ... but it won't write your email.

Sign up for your free extras by clicking on the QR code below or heading to the website we just mentioned and you'll be added to our newsletter list where you'll be the first to hear about all things connected to the world of unignorability.

POSTSCRIPT

There are a few people we have to thank for making this book possible.

The first thank you goes to all of our clients who pointed out that badly crafted emails are their first barrier to entering any vital conversation.

Equal gratitude goes out to Simon Pannatier, Georgie Peake, Vicky Hayhurst, Sarah-Jane Spooner and Thomas Hull who read the book in beta form and suggested some truly insightful additions.

Jayr Cuario is the one who made the whole thing as beautiful as it is.

Debbie Jenkins is the person we thank on a daily basis for persuading us to put fingers to keyboards and get our ideas into book form.

And where would we be without our amazing team of Email Evangelists. Thank you to Mark, Lee, Tim, Jane, Gordon, Chris, Marta and Niamh.

Last but not least, a big thank you to Sarah, who in case you didn't notice "wrote" all the before and after emails you have read in this book.

You'll be pleased to hear that with her new found unignorable skills she has now been poached by another organisation for a massive promotion and a ridiculously large salary.

DISCOVER MORE ABOUT THE DNA

If you'd like to know more about the ideas in *"The Art of the Unignorable Email"* you will find everything you need in *"The DNA of Engagement® - a story-based approach to building trust and influencing change".*

In 166 pages plus a downloadable workbook that we call the Rehearsal Notes you will discover how to:

- Master the foundations of trust
- Harness the secrets of narrative structure
- Build messages that stick
- Combine logic and emotion
- Tell stories that get people saying, "So, what happened next?"
- Foster collaboration and innovation

Follow this link to get your copy in paperback or on Kindle. And let us know what you think.[1]

https://geni.us/TheDNA

Leanne Hughes

⭐⭐⭐⭐⭐ **The most memorable and valuable framework around!**
Reviewed in the United States on 21 October 2024
Verified Purchase

DNA: Do Not Avoid this masterful book! You'll find yourself reading it, returning to it, and relying on it every time you need to influence minds and create lasting change. The framework is smart, the examples are punchy, and it's a fun read, too.

J Dillon

⭐⭐⭐⭐⭐ **Art of the story...**
Reviewed in the United Kingdom on 17 October 2024
Verified Purchase

The beauty of the book is that you can pick it up over and over again. And I will. When you feel like it's hard to reach your audience or you wonder how you can connect with people, this book will help you no end for sure. One for the 'book-it' list.

Suzy

⭐⭐⭐⭐⭐ **This is a GAME CHANGER.**
Reviewed in the United Kingdom on 17 October 2024
Verified Purchase

Effective communication is crucial at every career stage, but for those of us kicking off our journey, this book is like wielding a megaphone that ensures our voices are still heard and giving us the power to drive change from the get-go!

ENDNOTES

1   There's also a downloadable Secret Bonus Chapter that outlines all the
     DNA inversions we have discovered through working with our clients

MEET "THE STORY SPOTTERS"

David Pullan and Sarah Jane McKechnie met in a basement rehearsal room over thirty years ago. Before their second cup of tea they had decided that they'd found the person who was going to get them through the gruelling six-month tour of a "thriller without thrills" that lay ahead.

The years since then have been an amazing journey along roads that neither of them suspected were out there.

- Her first film was with Shirley MacLaine in an idyllic country house. Her last film was in an abandoned hospital smelling of wet socks. From "I've arrived!" to "I need a tetanus shot."

- He performed to Henry Kissinger and his security entourage and watched a young Robert Downey Jr. dance on a table in front of him. From international diplomacy to "get your shoes out of my dinner Tony Stark."

- Together they created a storytelling show where they cooked a chicken for the audience in real time.

It's been a life full of spotting, shaping and sharing the stories that surround all of us all the time.

And now, through their company The Story Spotters, they combine their experiences as performers, coaches, scriptwriters and hypnotherapists to help their clients master the communication moments that matter through the science, art and craft of story.

They also promise to respond to your emails.

You can find out more at www.thestoryspotters.com

All that is left is to quote the words of Mr Burns from The Simpsons Season 5 Episode 9 *The Last Temptation of Homer*, "Fly, my pretties. Fly!"

MORE PRAISE FOR THE ART OF THE UNIGNORABLE EMAIL

Real-world examples, laugh-out-loud-moments and clear, actionable steps. This book is as enjoyable to read as it is effective to apply at every level. Keep it on your desk.

Debbie Jenkins - The Expert's Publisher

Ignore this friendly book at your peril! I'd personally like the world to read it so I could get emails that shared my dream (understood me), helped me avoid nightmares (because as a business director I can't afford those) and provided a clear call to action all wrapped in a bundle that is definitely NOT TL;DR. Do yourself and your readers a huge service and grab this book.

- Dr Emma Williams, Researcher Development Consultant - EJW Solutions

Witty, psychologically sharp, and brilliantly useful. This is your secret weapon for making your emails stand out from the vanilla and AI-generated fluff that's flooding today's groaning inboxes. Another gem from David and Sarah Jane.

Jane Montgomery - Positive Psychology Practitioner

These frameworks will take your messages from 'straight to trash' to 'can't stop reading'. They might even make you the favourite in someone's inbox.

Tim Newman - The Recovering College Professor

Straight talking and easy to follow. The templates are genius. I've tried them and they work!

Jess Flack – Digital Inclusion Officer
- Essex County Council

This book is a roadmap for clear, human communication in a noisy world. Whether you lead, coach, sell or seek work, there's gold here for you.

- Gordon Rhodes - Career Whisperer - helping people find their pathway to purpose and possibility.

Read this book if you want to send messages that hit the mark. Your emails can influence, spur action, coordinate or inform if you just follow these simple and practical techniques.

Dan Kowalski - Solution Instigator
- Plan A Thinking

This book is the antidote to the email clutter we all dread. If you've ever stared at a blank screen, this is the book that will get your words working.

Prina Shah - author of
Make Work Meaningful

www.ingramcontent.com/pod-product-compliance
Lightning Source LLC
Chambersburg PA
CBHW040927210326
41597CB00030B/5204